The route to your roots

When they look back at their formative years, many Indians nostalgically recall the vital part Amar Chitra Katha picture books have played in their lives. It was **ACK – Amar Chitra Katha** – that first gave them a glimpse of their glorious heritage.

Since they were introduced in 1967, there are now **over 400 Amar Chitra Katha** titles to choose from. **Over 90 million copies** have been sold worldwide.

Now the Amar Chitra Katha titles are even more widely available in **1000+ bookstores all across India.** Log on to www.ack-media.com to locate a bookstore near you. If you do not have access to a bookstore, you can buy all the titles through our online store **www.amarchitrakatha.com.** We provide quick delivery anywhere in the world.

To make it easy for you to locate the titles of your choice from our treasure trove of titles, the books are now arranged in five categories.

Epics and Mythology
Best known stories from the Epics and the Puranas

Indian Classics
Enchanting tales from Indian literature

Fables and Humour
Evergreen folktales, legends and tales of wisdom and humour

Bravehearts
Stirring tales of brave men and women of India

Visionaries
Inspiring tales of thinkers, social reformers and nation builders

Amar Chitra Katha Pvt Ltd

© Amar Chitra Katha Pvt Ltd, 1999, Reprinted March 2012, ISBN 978-81-89999-19-3
Published & Printed by Amar Chitra Katha Pvt. Ltd., The Forum, 3rd Floor,
Raghuvanshi Mill Compound, S.B.Marg, Lower Parel (W), Mumbai- 400 013. India
For Consumer Complaints Contact Tel : +91- 22 40497436
Email: customerservice@ack-media.com

The route to your roots

A BAG OF
GOLD COINS

The precious bag contains the fruits of a lifetime of hard work. Thieves and scoundrels lay claim to it, but foolishness and downright dishonesty thwart their aspirations. As these tales reveal, fate eventually favours only the honest. The stories in this Amar Chitra Katha have been adapted from the *Anwar-i-Suhaili*, a Persian version of the Panchatantra, written by Hussain Ali Waiz in the 15th century. The tales were beautifully illustrated by famous artists in the court of Akbar and Jahangir.

Script	**Illustrations**	**Editor**
Shanti Devi Motichandra	V.B.Halbe	Anant Pal

A BAG OF GOLD COINS

LONG, LONG AGO THERE LIVED A FARMER WHO ALWAYS WORKED HARD.

WITH HIS TOIL, HE RAISED A BUMPER CROP.

AT LAST MY LABOUR HAS BEEN REWARDED!

HE THEN OPENED THE DOOR. IT WAS A FRIEND OF HIS OUTSIDE.

I AM ON MY WAY TO THE MARKET. I THOUGHT YOU MIGHT LIKE TO JOIN ME.

I CERTAINLY WOULD!

AS HE WAS SETTING OUT, HE SAW HIS WIFE.

I'LL BE BACK BY NOON. KEEP LUNCH READY.

IN HIS HURRY HE FORGOT ALL ABOUT THE BAG OF COINS.

WHEN HIS WIFE ENTERED THE KITCHEN—

THERE ISN'T A DROP OF WATER IN THE HOUSE. I MUST FETCH SOME.

SHE TOOK A POT...

THE UNGRATEFUL GOLDSMITH

ONCE UPON A TIME, A TRAVELLER WAS PASSING THROUGH A FOREST.

SUDDENLY—

HELP! HELP!

WHO IS THAT CALLING OUT FOR HELP?

HELP! HELP!

THE VOICE IS FROM THAT WELL. SOMEBODY MUST HAVE FALLEN IN.

O GOOD MAN, HELP US OUT OF THIS WELL.

THE KIND-HEARTED TRAVELLER LOWERED A CREEPER INTO THE WELL...

...AND PULLED THE ANIMALS UP.

I CAN'T LEAVE HIM TO DIE OF STARVATION. I WILL HELP HIM OUT.

WE WISH YOU WOULD HEED OUR ADVICE.

SOON THE MAN TOO WAS OUT OF THE WELL.

I AM A GOLDSMITH. YOU MUST VISIT ME AT MY HOUSE IN THE CITY.

A YEAR LATER, THE TRAVELLER RETURNED TO THE SAME SPOT WITH A BAG OF GOLD COINS.

IT IS GETTING DARK. LET ME REST NOW. TOMORROW I SHALL SEEK MY FRIENDS.

AS HE SLEPT, A BAND OF ROBBERS HAPPENED TO PASS BY.

THEY TIED HIM UP...

...PUSHED HIM DOWN THE EDGE OF A PRECIPICE...

...AND RAN AWAY WITH HIS BAG OF GOLD COINS.

AT THAT MOMENT, THE MONKEY WHO HAPPENED TO BE NEAR BY, HEARD SOMEONE CRYING FOR HELP.

THAT VOICE SOUNDS FAMILIAR. LET ME SEE WHO IT IS.

HELP! HELP!

AH! IT'S YOU! DO NOT WORRY, MY FRIEND. I'LL SET YOU FREE IN NO TIME.

FORTUNATELY FOR THE TRAVELLER, HE HAD FALLEN ON A HEAP OF GRASS.

THE MONKEY RESCUED HIM.

AS HE RESTED UNDER A TREE, THE TRAVELLER TOLD HIS TALE.

YOU STAY HERE AND RELAX. I'LL BRING YOU YOUR BAG OF GOLD COINS.

IT DID NOT TAKE THE MONKEY LONG TO FIND THE ROBBERS.

GOOD! THEY ARE ALL ASLEEP.

HE TOOK THEIR POSSESSIONS AND HID THEM IN A BUSH NEAR BY.

WHEN THE ROBBERS WOKE UP—

HEY! OUR SWORDS! OUR BOXES! WHERE ARE THEY?

SOME EVIL SPIRIT HAS WHISKED THEM AWAY.

THE JUBILANT MONKEY CARRIED THE BAG OF COINS TO THE TRAVELLER.

HERE IS YOUR BAG OF COINS.

YOU HAVE BEEN KIND TO ME, MY FRIEND.

THE TRAVELLER TOOK THE BAG OF COINS AND WENT ON HIS WAY. BUT SOON—

GRRR...

OH, GOD! A LION!

WHEN HE REACHED THE CITY, THE NEXT MORNING—

OUR PRINCESS IS KILLED!

DO YOU KNOW WHO DID IT?

IT IS HARD TO FIND SOMEONE IN THIS EXCITED CROWD WHO WILL GUIDE ME TO THE GOLDSMITH.

FORTUNATELY THE GOLDSMITH ALSO HAPPENED TO BE IN THAT CROWD.

MY FRIEND, IT IS A PLEASURE TO MEET YOU AGAIN. PLEASE COME HOME WITH ME.

I AM GLAD THAT YOU REMEMBER ME.

THE GOLDSMITH TOOK HIM HOME.

NOW WHAT CAN I DO FOR YOU?

I HAVE A NECKLACE, A PRESENT FROM OUR FRIEND, THE LION. HELP ME SELL IT AT A GOOD PRICE.

25

NO ONE WILL BE ABLE TO CURE HER OF MY POISON. THEN YOU GO TO THE PALACE...

...AND SAVE HER WITH THIS HERB. THE KING IS BOUND TO REWARD YOU.

GIVING HIM THE HERB, THE SNAKE WENT AWAY.

AFTER A WHILE, AT THE PALACE—

I'VE BEEN BITTEN BY A SNAKE! SAVE ME!

THE LEARNED MEN OF MEDICINE ALL CAME THERE.

WE HAVE TRIED ALL THE REMEDIES KNOWN TO US BUT IN VAIN, YOUR MAJESTY.

THE KING TURNED TO THE TRAVELLER.

PLEASE ACCEPT THIS BAG OF GOLD COINS.

THANK YOU, YOUR MAJESTY.

BY THEN IT WAS DAYBREAK. THE GOLDSMITH WAS WAITING AT THE PLACE OF EXECUTION.

THE TRAVELLER HAS NOT YET BEEN BROUGHT. ONCE HE IS HANGED, I'M SAFE.

JUST THEN THE KING'S SOLDIERS CAME THERE AND SEIZED HIM.

YOU ARE THE GUILTY ONE! YOU ARE TO BE HANGED! THE KING'S ORDERS.

MORAL: EVIL IS ALWAYS REWARDED WITH EVIL.

"5 brave brothers fought against their 100 cousins."

The 5 brothers won.

If the **Mahabharata** could be as simple,
it wouldn't have been an epic.

CHOICE OF FRIENDS

TALES FROM THE HITOPADESHA

The route to your roots

CHOICE
OF FRIENDS

Narayana, the author of these parables, insists that we exercise caution when choosing our companions. His charming animal characters – sometimes silly, sometimes wise – remind us of ourselves. We learn to avoid the pitfalls of life, along with his animal characters, thus attaining wisdom in a rather enjoyable way! Most importantly, we realise the worth of an honest friend.

Script
Kamala Chandakant

Illustrations
Jeffrey Fowler

Editor
Anant Pai

CHOICE OF FRIENDS

ONE DAY AT BREAK OF DAWN, A CROW PERCHED ON A TREE NEAR THE RIVER GODAVARI, SAW A FOWLER APPROACHING.

O LORD! HERE COMES YAMA* IN PERSON. I WONDER WHAT HE IS UP TO.

THE FOWLER FIXED HIS NET...

* THE·GOD OF DEATH.

1

* FOR STORY SEE PAGE 14

4

5

THE MOUSE DID HOLD OUT. HIS FRIEND'S NOBILITY GAVE HIM THE STRENGTH.

AS SOON AS YOU ARE FREE, YOU MUST LET ME TREAT YOU AND YOUR FOLLOWERS TO A FEAST.

A TRUE FRIEND INDEED. I WILL MAKE HIM MY FRIEND TOO.

THEN, THANKING THE MOUSE, THE PIGEON AND HIS FOLLOWERS FLEW AWAY.

AS THE MOUSE WAS ABOUT TO GO BACK TO HIS RETREAT, THE CROW FLEW DOWN TO HIM.

O STAUNCH FRIEND, LET ME TOO BE YOUR FRIEND.

.MOUSE

THE MOUSE WAS AMUSED.

HOW CAN THAT BE? I AM YOUR NATURAL FOOD. THE NEXT THING I KNOW, YOU WILL BE EATING ME. WE CAN NEVER BE FRIENDS.

BUT AT THE END OF IT—

YOU NEED HAVE NO FEAR OF THAT. YOU ARE TOO TINY TO BE EVEN A FULL BREAKFAST FOR ME.

A. MOU

AND THE MOUSE TOLD HIM THE STORY OF THE DEER, THE JACKAL AND THE CROW.*

* FOR STORY SEE PAGE 19

7

11

12

13

THE TIGER AND THE TRAVELLER

ONE DAY A TIGER, TOO OLD TO HUNT, WAS WALKING BY A MARSHY POOL WHEN HE SAW A GOLD BANGLE.

I MAY AS WELL PICK IT UP. IT COULD BE OF SOME USE.

I'VE GOT THE BAIT. NOW I MUST WAIT FOR THE CATCH.

JUST THEN A TRAVELLER PASSED BY THE OPPOSITE BANK.

15

16

17

THE CROW, THE DEER AND THE JACKAL

LONG, LONG AGO THERE LIVED A DEER AND A CROW. THEY WERE GOOD FRIENDS AND LOVED EACH OTHER DEARLY.

ONE DAY A JACKAL SAW THE DEER.

WHAT A DELICIOUS MEAL HE WOULD MAKE. MM-M-M!

HE WENT UP TO THE DEER.

GOOD DAY, MY FRIEND.

WHO ARE YOU?

NO! DEAR FRIEND, I SHALL WAIT WITH YOU TILL THE END. PERHAPS I MIGHT STILL SAVE YOU.

THE CROW RACKED HIS BRAINS BUT COULD FIND NO WAY OUT. AT LAST DAY BROKE.

ALAS! THERE COMES THE FARMER WITH HIS CLUB. IF ONLY I COULD THINK OF SOME MEANS TO SAVE MY FRIEND.

SUDDENLY AN IDEA STRUCK HIM.

I HAVE IT! LIE ON YOUR BACK, PUFF YOUR STOMACH OUT, STIFFEN YOUR LEGS AND BE VERY STILL. I WILL PECK AT YOUR EYES. THEN WHEN I CROAK, SPRING TO YOUR FEET AND RUN FOR YOUR LIFE.

THE DEER DID EXACTLY AS HE WAS TOLD. WHEN THE FARMER CAME UP TO HIM —

AHA! THE FELLOW IS DEAD — OF FRIGHT NO DOUBT. WELL, THAT MAKES MY TASK EASIER.

HE BEGAN REMOVING THE NET.

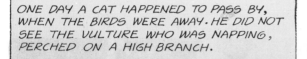

ONE DAY A CAT HAPPENED TO PASS BY, WHEN THE BIRDS WERE AWAY. HE DID NOT SEE THE VULTURE WHO WAS NAPPING, PERCHED ON A HIGH BRANCH.

AHA! NESTS AND NESTS OF LITTLE FLEDGLINGS. FOOD ENOUGH FOR DAYS AND DAYS.

WHEN THE LITTLE BIRDS SAW THE CAT APPROACH, THEY SET UP SUCH A TWITTER THAT THE VULTURE WOKE UP.

HE SWOOPED DOWN.

WHO GOES THERE?

A VULTURE! OH! OH! I'M DONE FOR!

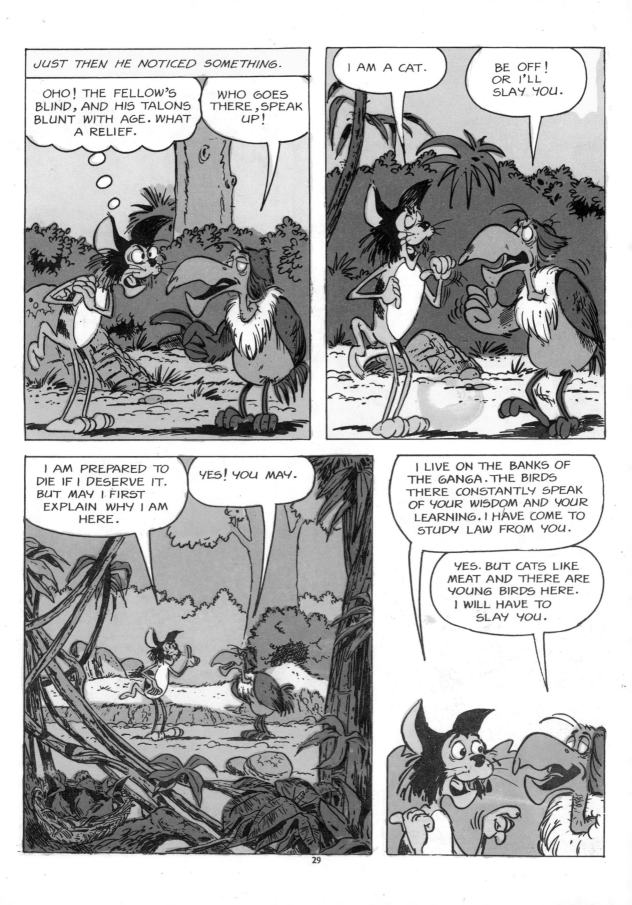

HOW FRIENDS ARE PARTED

TALES FROM THE HITOPADESHA

The route to your roots

HOW FRIENDS
ARE PARTED

Hitopadesha is a collection of ancient Sanskrit fables written by Narayana Pandit. It is dated around 11th or 12th century AD. The four stories chosen in this group have simple moral tales to tell. Lions, jackals, monkeys, cats, dogs and donkeys are protagonists who teach common sense lessons in how to judge for oneself; how not to succumb to rumourmongers; how to mind one's own business and how not to be greedy.

Script
The Editorial Team

Illustrations
Ashok Dongre

Editor
Anant Pai

IN THE SAME FOREST WERE TWO JACKALS, DAMANAKA AND KARATAKA, WHO WERE FAR FROM HAPPY.

WE HAVE FALLEN FROM KING LION'S FAVOUR. NO MORE FEASTS FOR US!

WE DON'T HAVE TO STARVE. WE CAN HUNT, CAN'T WE?

JUST THEN KING LION PASSED BY WITHOUT EVEN GLANCING AT THE TWO JACKALS.

KARATAKA, MARK MY WORDS. BY OUR EFFORTS WE WILL WIN BACK THE CONFIDENCE OF OUR KING.

THE LION APPROACHED A POOL OF WATER.

THAT WAS A GRAND FEAST. NOW FOR A LONG DEEP DRINK OF WATER. THEN ... SLEEP!

EVEN AS THE LION BEGAN TO DRINK ...

3

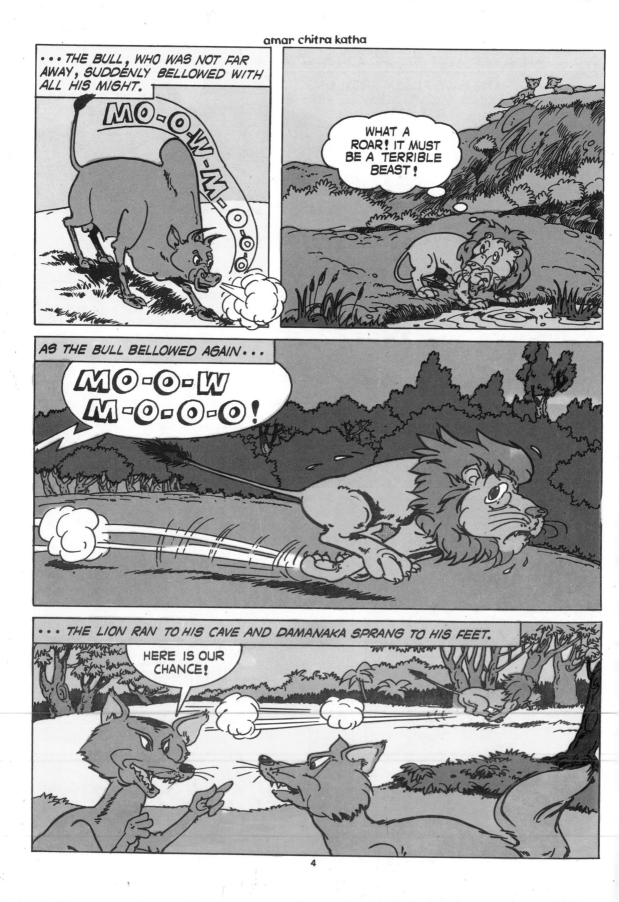

6

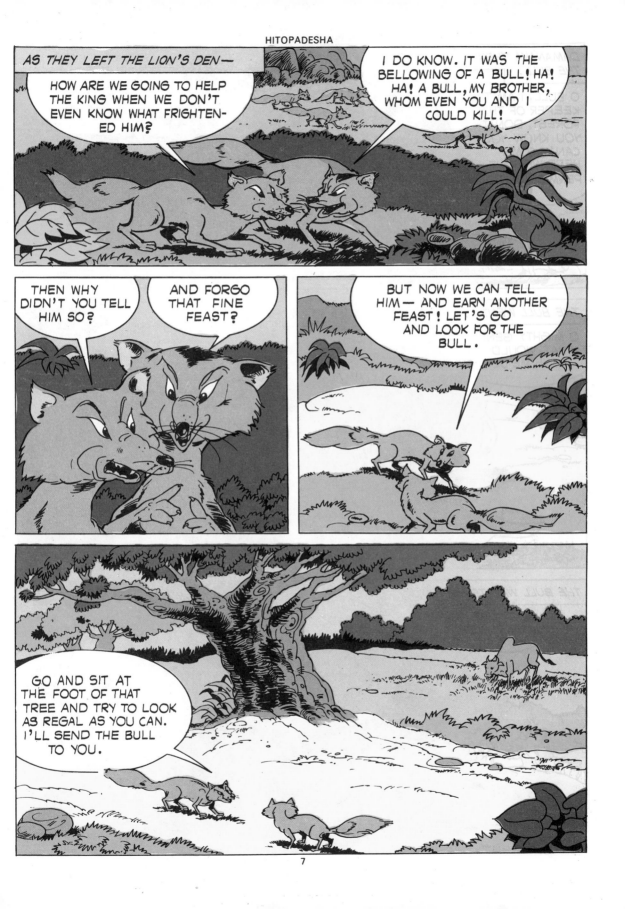

7

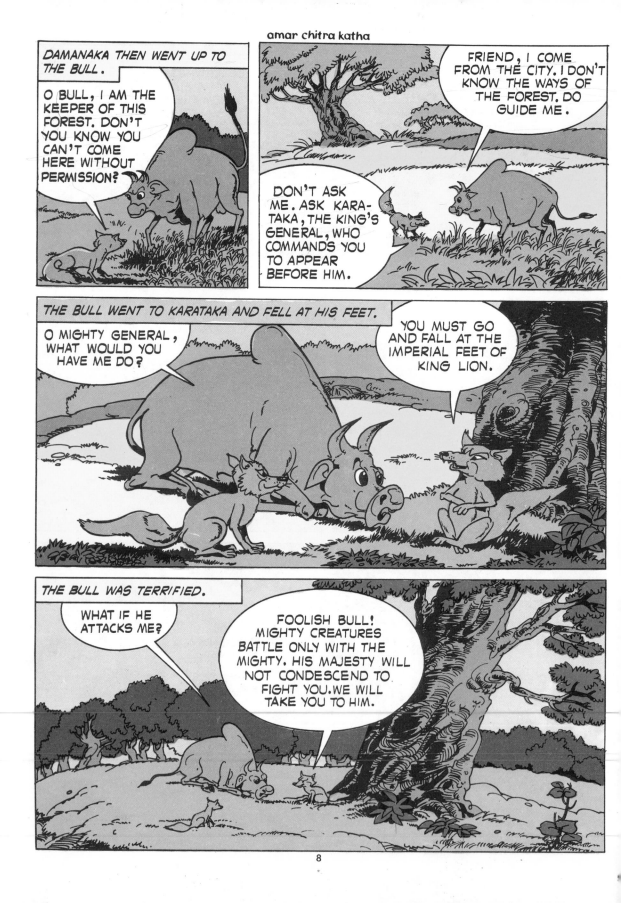

DAMANAKA THEN WENT UP TO THE BULL.

O BULL, I AM THE KEEPER OF THIS FOREST. DON'T YOU KNOW YOU CAN'T COME HERE WITHOUT PERMISSION?

FRIEND, I COME FROM THE CITY. I DON'T KNOW THE WAYS OF THE FOREST. DO GUIDE ME.

DON'T ASK ME. ASK KARATAKA, THE KING'S GENERAL, WHO COMMANDS YOU TO APPEAR BEFORE HIM.

THE BULL WENT TO KARATAKA AND FELL AT HIS FEET.

O MIGHTY GENERAL, WHAT WOULD YOU HAVE ME DO?

YOU MUST GO AND FALL AT THE IMPERIAL FEET OF KING LION.

THE BULL WAS TERRIFIED.

WHAT IF HE ATTACKS ME?

FOOLISH BULL! MIGHTY CREATURES BATTLE ONLY WITH THE MIGHTY. HIS MAJESTY WILL NOT CONDESCEND TO FIGHT YOU. WE WILL TAKE YOU TO HIM.

DAMANAKA RETURNED TO HIS BROTHER AND THE TWO OF THEM LED THE BULL TO THE LION.

YOUR MAJESTY, I COME TO PAY YOU HOMAGE.

COME, COME, MY GOOD FRIEND! WE ARE EQUALS. ONLY A SUB-ORDINATE PAYS HOMAGE TO A SUPERIOR.

BE MY GUEST AND LIVE AS LONG AS YOU LIKE IN MY FOREST.

THE BULL WAS PLEASANTLY SURPRISED. HE CONTINUED LIVING IN THE FOREST, NOW AS THE HONOURED GUEST OF HIS MAJESTY, THE LION.

ONE DAY THE LION CAME UP TO THE BULL WITH ANOTHER LION.

FRIEND, PLEASE LOOK AFTER MY BROTHER WHILE I GO AND HUNT FOR SOME FOOD FOR HIM.

BUT, YOUR MAJESTY, WHAT ABOUT THE FLESH OF ALL THE ANIMALS THAT WERE SLAIN TODAY?

15

THE BULL, MEANWHILE, HAD COME NEAR THE DEN.

THE JACKAL WAS RIGHT. HIS MAJESTY HAS CRUEL INTENTIONS. I WILL NOT DIE WITHOUT A FIGHT.

HE LOWERED HIS HORNS AND CHARGED.

THE LION SOON KILLED HIM. AS HE STOOD STARING AT THE CARCASS OF THE BULL, A WEIRD SOUND CAUGHT HIS EARS.

HE! HE! HE!
HE! HE! HE!

WHAT'S THAT I HEAR? THE GLEEFUL HOWL OF THE JACKALS! AH, I HAVE LET THE CUNNING JACKALS OUTWIT ME AND PART ME FROM A TRUE FRIEND!

16

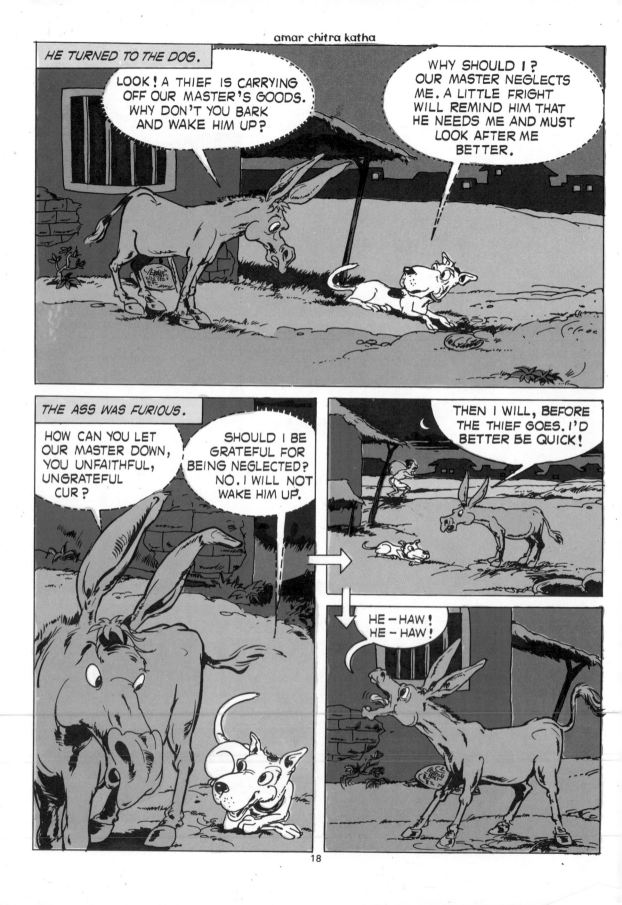

BUT THE CAT HAD BEEN TOO HASTY.

I NO LONGER HEAR THE LITTLE PEST MOVE ABOUT. SHE MUST HAVE GONE SOMEWHERE ELSE.

AS THE DAYS PASSED, THE LION NO LONGER NEEDING THE CAT'S SERVICES, DID NOT BOTHER TO FEED HIM.

FRIEND LION, I'M HUNGRY.

THEN GO AND CATCH YOURSELF SOME MICE. I'D LIKE TO SLEEP NOW. DON'T DISTURB ME.

THE CAT LEFT THE DEN, A WISER ANIMAL.

I'VE BEEN A FOOL! I SHOULD NOT HAVE KILLED THAT MOUSE.

28

IN THE FOREST SHE THREW THE MANGOES ABOUT...

IF MY GUESS IS RIGHT THE "DEMON" WILL COME OUT!

...AND HID BEHIND A TREE.

THE MONKEYS SMELT THE MANGOES AND CAME SCAMPERING UP.

MANGOES!

THE BELL WAS DROPPED IN THE DASH FOR THE MANGOES.

I WAS RIGHT! THERE'S NO DEMON HERE! ONLY SOME MONKEYS WITH A BELL!

COMING OUT FROM HER HIDING PLACE...

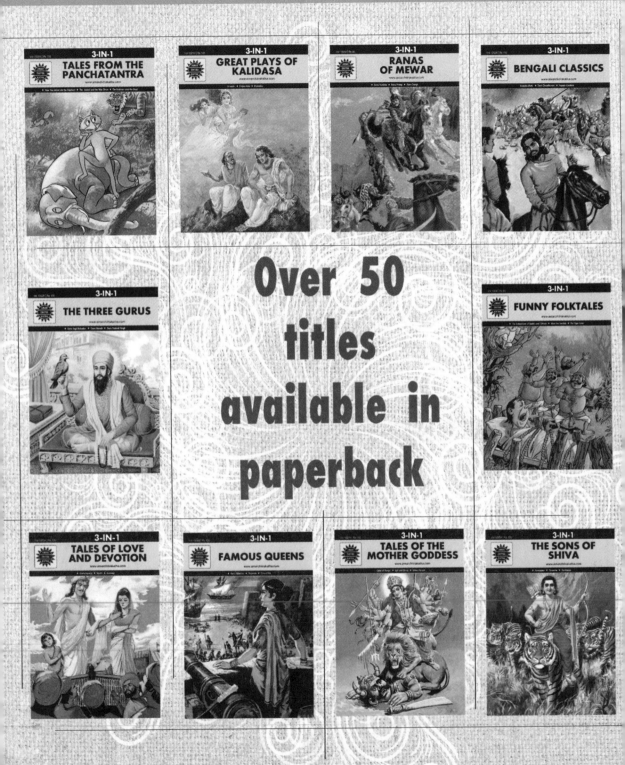

THE TIGER AND THE WOODPECKER

ANIMAL TALES FROM A TELUGU CLASSIC

The route to your roots

THE TIGER AND
THE WOODPECKER

Telugu, a vibrant language even in medieval times, produced the distinguished poet Manchana. His stories are all delightful lessons in wisdom. Some teach us the value of honour while others tell us that might is not always right. We see a tiny rat outwitting a venomous serpent and then an old turtle saving his friends from a greedy eagle. Read on to learn a trick or two...

Script
C.R.Sharma and
Kamala Chandrakant

Illustrations
Ashok Dongre

Editor
Anant Pai

THE WOODPECKER WAS PUZZLED.

WHAT'S THE MATTER WITH YOU? WHY DO YOU LIE THERE WITH YOUR MOUTH OPEN?

THE TIGER BECKONED TO THE WOODPECKER TO COME NEAR...

...AND POINTED TO THE BONE IN HIS MOUTH.

OH! OH! IT'S A BONE. I SHALL REMOVE IT...IF YOU WILL GIVE ME MY FILL OF THE FLESH OF THE ANIMALS YOU KILL.

THE TIGER NODDED HIS HEAD.

THE WOODPECKER FLEW INTO THE TIGER'S MOUTH...

3

THE CLEVER TURTLE

LONG AGO, THERE LIVED A FEW TURTLES ON A SEA COAST. EVERY DAY AN EAGLE USED TO CATCH ONE OF THEM FOR FOOD.

THIS WORRIED AN AGED TURTLE.

AT THIS RATE, NOT ONE OF US WILL BE LEFT ALIVE.

WE MUST DO SOMETHING TO SAVE OURSELVES.

HE WITHDREW INTO HIS SHELL AND BEGAN TO THINK HARD.

WHY, THAT'S IT! WHY DIDN'T I THINK OF IT BEFORE!

6

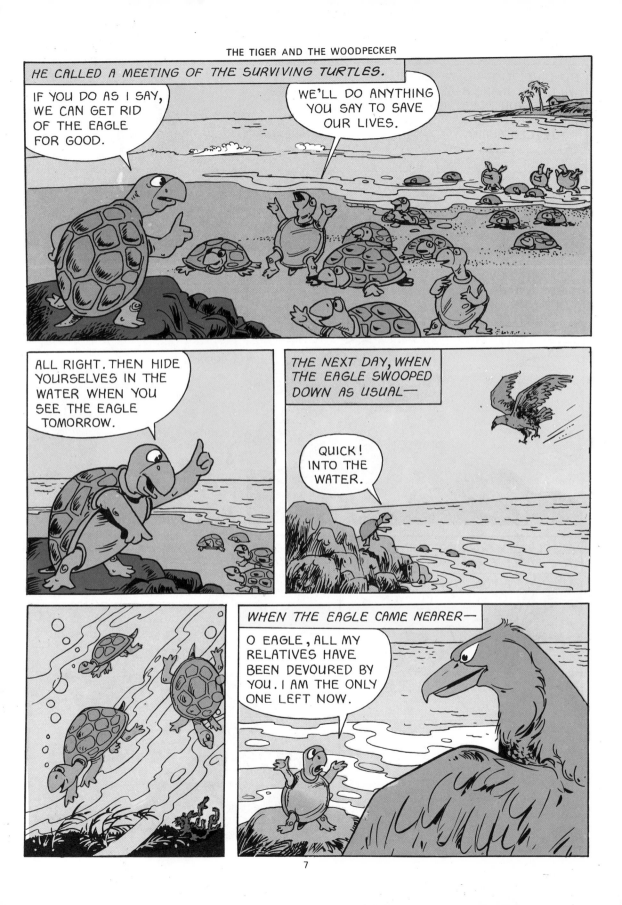

7

THE HARE, THE PARTRIDGE AND THE TIGER

ON THE BANKS OF THE NARMADA WAS A FOREST. THE ANIMALS WHO LIVED THERE WERE ALWAYS QUARRELLING.

WE QUARREL BECAUSE WE HAVE NO KING TO SETTLE OUR DISPUTES.

YES. WE SHOULD HAVE A KING.

BUT WHO WILL BE THE KING?

PANDEMONIUM BROKE OUT.

I WILL BE THE KING.

NOT YOU. I WILL BE THE KING.

IT SHOULD BE ME.

AN OLD AND INFIRM TIGER, WHO HAD RECENTLY MIGRATED TO THAT FOREST WAS ROUSED FROM HIS SLUMBER.

WHERE IS THIS NOISE FROM? LET ME SEE.

WHEN THE ANIMALS SAW THE OLD TIGER APPROACHING—

WHY DON'T WE MAKE HIM OUR KING?

A GOOD IDEA.

SO WHEN THE OLD TIGER CAME TO THEM—

WE NEED A KING. WILL YOU BE OUR KING AND RULE OVER US?

I CAN'T BELIEVE MY GOOD LUCK! MY DAYS OF STARVATION ARE OVER.

I DO NOT MIND BEING KING. BUT I DISLIKE VIOLENCE. SO I WILL KILL ONLY IF IT IS ABSOLUTELY NECESSARY, AFTER MAKING A CAREFUL STUDY OF EACH CASE.

THE ANIMALS WERE DELIGHTED.

O KING, WE TOO DISLIKE AND FEAR VIOLENCE. BUT A JUST KING HAS TO KILL THE GUILTY ONES.

AND MOST OF THE TIME I WILL FIND IT NECESSARY.

THE VERY NEXT DAY, A HARE AND A PARTRIDGE HAD A BITTER QUARREL.

THIS HOLE IS MINE.

NO, IT IS MINE! I FOUND IT FIRST.

YOU FOUND IT ALL RIGHT. BUT IT WAS MY FATHER WHO MADE IT.

BUT YOUR FATHER ABANDONED IT. I MOVED IN. SO IT'S MINE.

THE HARE WAS QUIET FOR A MOMENT. THEN AN IDEA STRUCK HIM.

LET'S GO TO OUR KING! LET HIM DECIDE TO WHOM IT BELONGS.

FAIR ENOUGH. WE'LL GO TO HIM.

14

THE SERPENT AND THE RAT

A SNAKE-CHARMER ONCE CAUGHT A SERPENT AND PUT IT INTO A CANE BASKET.

THEN HE CAUGHT A RAT AND PUT IT INTO THE BASKET, TOO.

THERE! THAT SHOULD MAKE A FINE MEAL FOR MY SERPENT.

BUT WHEN THE SERPENT CAME NEAR THE RAT TO EAT IT—

PLEASE SPARE MY LIFE! I CAN FREE YOU.

THE SERPENT WAS AMUSED.

HOW CAN YOU SUCCEED WHERE I HAVE FAILED. BESIDES, I'M TERRIBLY HUNGRY.

16

THE FOOLISH BRAHMAN

A LEARNED BRAHMAN NAMED GARGYA ONCE WENT FROM HIS VILLAGE TO A FOREST, TO WORSHIP GODDESS DURGA.

PLEASED WITH HIS DEVOTION, THE GODDESS APPEARED BEFORE HIM.

O PIOUS BRAHMAN, YOU DESERVE A BOON. ASK FOR ONE.

O GODDESS, PLEASE GRANT ME THE SANJEEVANI.*

THE GODDESS HELD OUT SOME GREEN LEAVES.

WHENEVER YOU WANT TO BRING THE DEAD BACK TO LIFE, ALL YOU NEED DO IS SPRINKLE THE SAP OF THESE LEAVES ON THE CORPSE.

THE BODY THUS RAISED WILL BE STRONGER AND MORE VIGOROUS THAN BEFORE.

✳ A HERB WHICH IS CREDITED WITH THE POWER TO REVIVE THE DEAD.

20

THE FEMALE PARROT AND THE HUNTER

ONE DAY, THE FEMALE PARROT LAID SOME EGGS...

...AND SAT TENDERLY ON THEM. UNKNOWN TO HER, A HUNTER WAS CAREFULLY WATCHING HER FROM ANOTHER TREE.

AH! SHE HAS MOVED FROM THE NEST. A GOOD SIGN.

THERE ONCE LIVED A FEMALE PARROT ON A BIG TREE IN A FOREST. IN THE HOLLOW OF ANOTHER TREE NEAR BY, LIVED A VENOMOUS SERPENT.

THEN ONE DAY THE HUNTER HEARD THE CHEEP OF FLEDGELINGS.

CHEEP CHEEP

THIS IS MY LUCKY DAY. THE EGGS HAVE HATCHED. THEY'LL FETCH A TIDY SUM.

25

THE FOOLISH CRANE

LONG AGO, THERE LIVED AN OLD CRANE NEAR A LAKE ON THE BANK OF WHICH WAS A TALL COCONUT TREE.

THE LAKE BEING ALMOST DRY, THERE WERE JUST ENOUGH FISH FOR THE CRANE TO LIVE ON. BUT THE OLD CRANE WAS VAIN ABOUT HIS TREE AND HIS LAKE.

HOW I WISH OTHER CRANES TOO WOULD COME AND SETTLE HERE AND SEE HOW LUCKY I AM.

THEN ONE DAY, HE SAW A FLOCK OF CRANES FLYING PAST HIS LAKE.

STOP! STOP. PLEASE STOP.

THE LEADER OF THE FLOCK SAW HIM.

THAT OLD BIRD IS CALLING OUT TO US. LET'S FLY DOWN AND SEE WHAT HE WANTS.

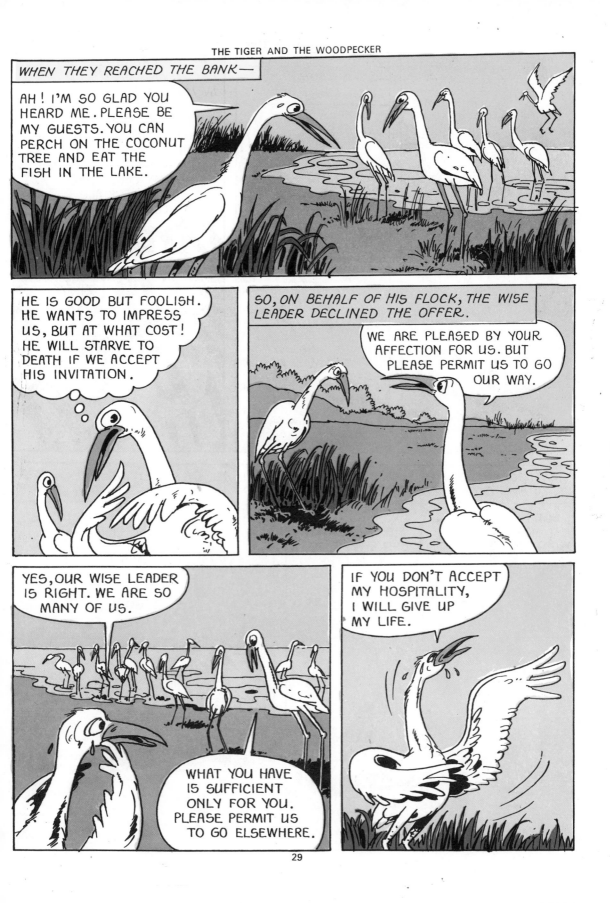

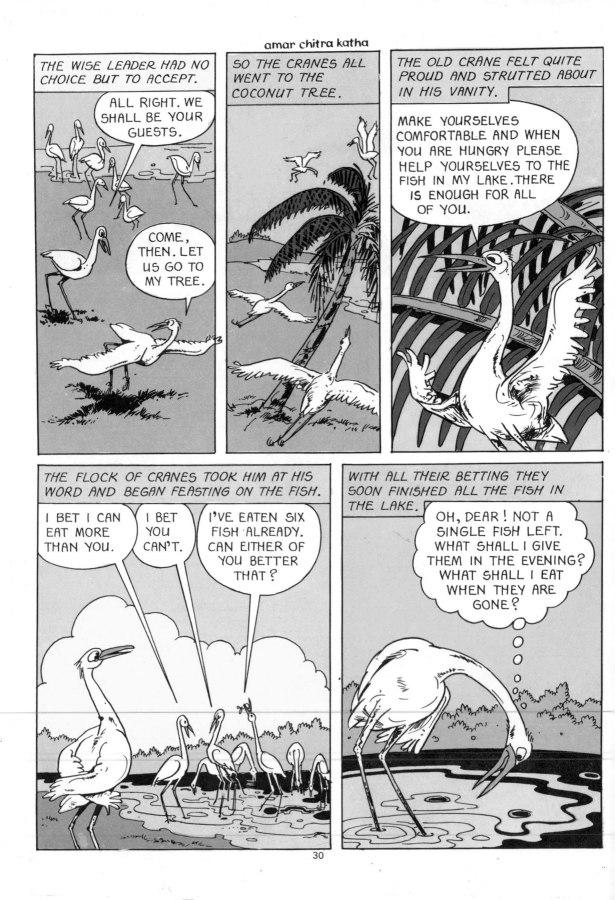

THE WISE LEADER HAD NO CHOICE BUT TO ACCEPT.

ALL RIGHT. WE SHALL BE YOUR GUESTS.

COME, THEN. LET US GO TO MY TREE.

SO THE CRANES ALL WENT TO THE COCONUT TREE.

THE OLD CRANE FELT QUITE PROUD AND STRUTTED ABOUT IN HIS VANITY.

MAKE YOURSELVES COMFORTABLE AND WHEN YOU ARE HUNGRY PLEASE HELP YOURSELVES TO THE FISH IN MY LAKE. THERE IS ENOUGH FOR ALL OF YOU.

THE FLOCK OF CRANES TOOK HIM AT HIS WORD AND BEGAN FEASTING ON THE FISH.

I BET I CAN EAT MORE THAN YOU.

I BET YOU CAN'T.

I'VE EATEN SIX FISH ALREADY. CAN EITHER OF YOU BETTER THAT?

WITH ALL THEIR BETTING THEY SOON FINISHED ALL THE FISH IN THE LAKE.

OH, DEAR! NOT A SINGLE FISH LEFT. WHAT SHALL I GIVE THEM IN THE EVENING? WHAT SHALL I EAT WHEN THEY ARE GONE?

THE OLD CRANE BEGAN TO REPENT OF HIS FOLLY BUT IT WAS TOO LATE. THAT EVENING THE LEADER OF THE FLOCK CAME TO HIM—

THERE IS NOTHING HERE FOR OUR EVENING MEAL. WE ARE GRATEFUL TO YOU FOR YOUR HOSPITALITY BUT WE MUST LEAVE NOW. I CANNOT LET MY FLOCK STARVE.

AS THEY FLEW AWAY, THE LEADER FELT SORRY FOR THE LONE CRANE NEAR THE LAKE.

HE'S TOO OLD TO FLY WITH US. IF ONLY HE HAD LISTENED TO US! POOR FOOL! HE WILL NOT SURVIVE FOR LONG.

A FEW DAYS LATER, WEAK AND HUNGRY, THE VAIN, OLD CRANE BREATHED HIS LAST.

THE END

FRIENDS AND FOES

ANIMAL TALES FROM THE MAHABHARATA

www.amarchitrakatha.com

AMAR CHITRA KATHA

The route to your roots

FRIENDS AND FOES

In the Mahabharata, when Yudhishthira asks Bheeshma what the right conduct of a king should be, the wise Bheeshma answers in the form of stories. Cats and mice, crows and swans, leopards and jackals, all serve to show how a king must deal in times of crisis, doubt or personal problems.

Script
Toni Patel

Illustrations
Pradeep Sathe

Editor
Anant Pai

2

HE LOOKED AROUND FOR A WAY TO ESCAPE AND GOT ANOTHER SHOCK— THERE WAS AN OWL ON THE TREE!

WHAT SHALL I DO?

IF I STAY HERE, THAT OWL WILL TEAR ME TO PIECES WITH HIS SHARP BEAK···

···BUT IF I TRY TO RUN AWAY THE MONGOOSE WILL SWALLOW ME UP!

ON EVERY SIDE THERE IS DANGER! DEATH ITSELF IS STARING ME IN THE FACE!

I THOUGHT I WAS LUCKY WHEN MY WORST ENEMY, LOMASHA, WAS ENSNARED. BUT, IN A WAY, HE PROTECTED ME FROM THE OTHERS BY HIS VERY PRESENCE.

AND NOW HE COULD DO WITH MY HELP... THAT'S IT! HE NEEDS ME AND I NEED HIM.

TURNING TO THE CAT, HE TALKED TO HIM WITH FRIENDLY CONCERN.

DEAR LOMASHA, I WISH TO HELP YOU. IF YOU AGREE TO DO THE SAME FOR ME, I WILL RELEASE YOU FROM YOUR PRESENT PLIGHT. WILL YOU LISTEN TO ME?

DO YOU REALLY MEAN TO HELP ME? A SHORT WHILE AGO YOU WERE REJOICING AT MY MISFORTUNE!

THINGS ARE DIFFERENT NOW. I THOUGHT OF YOU AS MY ONLY ENEMY BUT I HAD FORGOTTEN ABOUT THE MONGOOSE AND THE OWL.

LOOK, THERE THEY ARE, WAITING TO POUNCE UPON ME!

MEANWHILE, THE MONGOOSE HAD HIS EYES FIXED ON PALITA.

A RAT IN THE ARMS OF A CAT! I'VE NEVER SEEN ANYTHING LIKE IT IN MY LIFE!

ANYWAY, I CAN'T WAIT HERE FOREVER. I'LL FIND SOMETHING ELSE TO EAT!

GOOD! HE'S GOING AWAY!

PRETTY SOON THE OWL, TOO, GAVE UP.

IT WILL SOON BE DAYBREAK. I'D BETTER LOOK FOR ANOTHER PREY!

AFTER THIS, PALITA BEGAN TO CUT THE STRINGS OF THE NET WITH HIS SHARP TEETH.

O, WISE BEING! THROUGH YOUR GRACE, I HAVE ALMOST GOT BACK MY LIFE!

BUT PALITA, IN ACCORDANCE WITH HIS OWN PLANS, WORKED VERY SLOWLY.

DEAR FRIEND, DON'T WASTE TIME. DO CUT THESE STRINGS QUICKLY! IT WILL SOON BE DAWN AND THE HUNTER WILL BE HERE!

PATIENCE! ALL IN GOOD TIME!

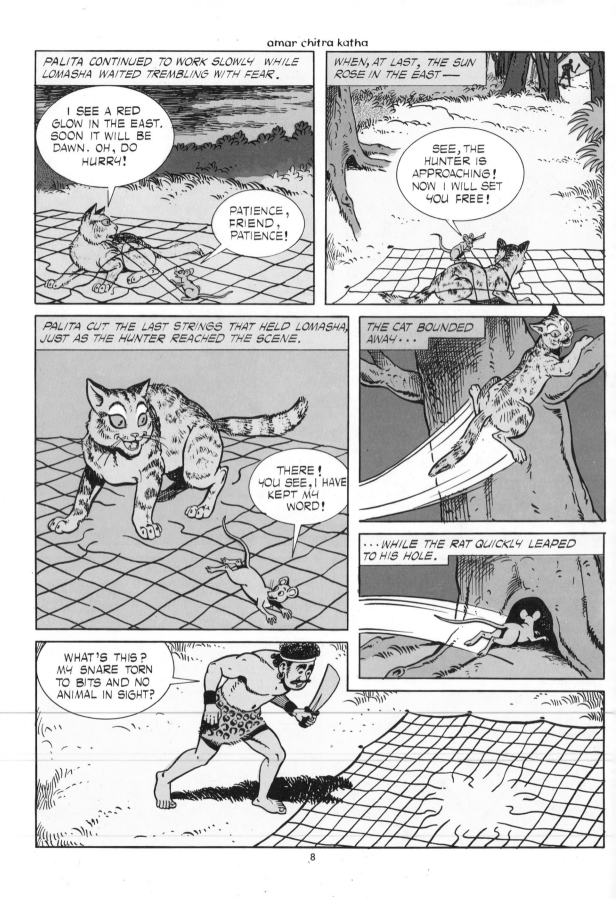

PALITA CONTINUED TO WORK SLOWLY WHILE LOMASHA WAITED TREMBLING WITH FEAR.

I SEE A RED GLOW IN THE EAST. SOON IT WILL BE DAWN. OH, DO HURRY!

PATIENCE, FRIEND, PATIENCE!

WHEN, AT LAST, THE SUN ROSE IN THE EAST—

SEE, THE HUNTER IS APPROACHING! NOW I WILL SET YOU FREE!

PALITA CUT THE LAST STRINGS THAT HELD LOMASHA, JUST AS THE HUNTER REACHED THE SCENE.

THERE! YOU SEE, I HAVE KEPT MY WORD!

THE CAT BOUNDED AWAY...

...WHILE THE RAT QUICKLY LEAPED TO HIS HOLE.

WHAT'S THIS? MY SNARE TORN TO BITS AND NO ANIMAL IN SIGHT?

WHEN THE PUZZLED HUNTER HAD GONE AWAY, THE CAT ADDRESSED HIS NEW-FOUND FRIEND.

OH, PALITA, I AM VERY GRATEFUL TO YOU FOR SAVING MY LIFE! LET THERE BE PEACE BETWEEN US ALWAYS! I WILL ASK ALL MY KINSMEN AND FRIENDS NOT TO HURT YOU.

BUT THE RAT WAS WISE.

YOU ARE MISTAKEN, O LOMASHA! THERE ARE TIMES WHEN SELF-INTEREST CAN MAKE A FOE A FRIEND. BUT SOONER OR LATER THEY WILL BECOME ENEMIES.

NO, NO. NOT IF ONE OF THEM HAS SAVED THE OTHER'S LIFE!

IT IS POSSIBLE YOU ARE PRETENDING TO BE MY FRIEND — JUST TO CATCH ME THE MORE EASILY!

PLEASE, LISTEN TO ME···

NO, LOMASHA, GO YOUR WAY — AND KEEP YOUR DISTANCE FROM THE EVIL HUNTER!

THE CAT SHIVERED ON HEARING THE WORD 'HUNTER' AND MADE HASTE TO RUN AWAY.

THE TIGER AND THE JACKAL

DEEP IN THE JUNGLES OF THE HIMALAYAS, THERE WAS A JACKAL WHO LIVED THE LIFE OF A RECLUSE.

THIS JACKAL WAS COMPASSIONATE AND TRUTHFUL WHEREAS HIS COMPANIONS WERE CRUEL AND RAPACIOUS.

WHAT STRANGE BEHAVIOUR IS THIS? ONE WOULD THINK HE WAS AN ASCETIC PRACTISING AUSTERITIES!

AND WE JACKALS RELISH FLESH.

SUCH BEHAVIOUR IS PERVERSE! EVERY ONE MUST REMAIN TRUE TO HIS NATURE!

LET'S GO AND GIVE HIM A BIT OF ADVICE.

LOOK, FRIEND, THE WAY IN WHICH YOU LIVE WON'T DO! WE DON'T LIKE IT!

ALL OF US WILL GIVE YOU MEAT. YOU DON'T HAVE TO LIVE LIKE AN ASCETIC!

THANK YOU FOR YOUR KIND CONCERN, BUT I AM QUITE HAPPY LIVING ON FRUIT.

HA! DO YOU IMAGINE THAT BY IMITATING A HIGHER CASTE YOU CAN CHANGE YOUR POSITION IN SOCIETY?

THE TIGER WHO WAS EAVESDROPPING WAS THE KING OF THE FOREST. HE DREW NEAR AS SOON AS THE OTHERS HAD LEFT.

O RIGHTEOUS PERSON! I HEARD EVERY WORD YOU UTTERED. I RESPECT YOU FOR SUCH HONOURABLE SENTIMENTS!

PLEASE COME TO MY COURT AND BE MY CHIEF MINISTER.

I THANK YOU FOR YOUR OFFER, O MIGHTY KING, BUT...

...I DO NOT WANT LUXURY SUCH AS COURT LIFE AFFORDS. I HAVE NEVER SERVED ANOTHER. I AM QUITE HAPPY WHERE I AM.

HOWEVER, IF YOU STILL WISH TO APPOINT ME, I WILL OBEY — PROVIDED YOU TREAT MY ADVICE WITH RESPECT AND ALLOW ME TO GIVE IT TO YOU IN PRIVATE.

I GLADLY AGREE TO YOUR CONDITIONS!

SO THE JACKAL WENT TO THE COURT AND WAS TREATED BY THE KING WITH GREAT RESPECT.

OH! SO THAT'S THE NEW CHIEF MINISTER.

OH! HE'S JUST ANOTHER JACKAL! IF WE CONFIDE IN HIM, HE'LL SOON DO US OUT OF EVERYTHING WE HAVE!

THEY SAY HE IS HONEST. SHOULD WE TALK TO HIM OF OUR TROUBLES?

BUT, GRADUALLY, THEY LEARNT TO TRUST HIM. ONE BY ONE, THEY CAME TO HIM WITH THEIR PROBLEMS.

MY SON WAS PUNISHED FOR STEALING. BUT HE WAS INNOCENT!

THEN WHO WAS THE REAL THIEF?

IT WAS ONE OF THE MAGISTRATE'S FRIENDS!

MY CHILDREN ARE STARVING AND WE HAVE NO FOOD STORED FOR THE RAINY SEASON!

HOW IS THAT? I KNOW YOUR HUSBAND WORKS HARD.

HE DOES NOT ALWAYS GET WORK BECAUSE THE JACKAL IN CHARGE WANTS A BRIBE FROM HIM!

THE JACKAL SOON SAW TO IT THAT THEY GOT JUSTICE. BUT THOSE WHO WERE EXPLOITING THE POOR ANIMALS WERE VERY ANGRY.

THAT MINISTER IS ONE OF US. WHY SHOULD HE SIDE WITH THE COMMON PEOPLE?

HE HAS DONE AN UNFORGIVABLE THING. HE HAS SET THE HARE FREE AND SENT OUR GOOD FRIEND, THE MAGISTRATE, TO JAIL!

IT WON'T DO! WE MUST GET RID OF HIM!

THEY LOOKED ABOUT FOR WAYS OF DISCREDITING HIM. ONE DAY —

LOOK AT THAT FRESH PIECE OF MEAT LAID OUT FOR THE KING!

TAKE IT AWAY AT ONCE AND PUT IT IN THE CHIEF MINISTER'S ROOM! LEAVE THE REST TO ME!

OH, THEY INTEND TO HARM HIM!

THE CHIEF MINISTER HAS ALWAYS BEFRIENDED ME. BUT HOW CAN I HELP HIM? I AM AFRAID THEY WILL HARM ME, TOO, IF I OBJECT!

15

16

SO THE JACKAL WHO WAS CHIEF MINISTER WAS PLACED UNDER ARREST.

SOON AFTER, THE KING'S MOTHER HEARD ABOUT IT AND HURRIED TO SPEAK TO HER SON.

THIS CANNOT BE TRUE! I AM CERTAIN THE CHIEF MINISTER IS INNOCENT, THE VICTIM OF SOME EVIL PLOT!

BUT, MOTHER, THE MEAT WAS IN HIS ROOM. I SAW IT WITH MY OWN EYES!

WHILE THEY WERE HOTLY DISCUSSING THE CASE, A JACKAL CAME IN.

O, KING, MAY I BE ALLOWED TO SPEAK? IT IS IMPORTANT!

THE CHIEF MINISTER IS INNOCENT! TO PLOT HIS DOWNFALL, MY FRIENDS LIED ABOUT HIM TO YOU!

YOU SEE! I TOLD YOU SO!

BUT WHY DID YOU NOT SPEAK UP BEFORE? WERE YOU NOT AMONG THE VILE JACKALS WHEN THEY TALKED TO ME A LITTLE WHILE AGO?

I REMAINED SILENT TO SAVE MY SKIN, FOR I WAS AFRAID OF THEM. BUT I PLEAD FOR YOUR GRACIOUS MERCY.

ALL RIGHT, YOU MAY GO THOUGH YOU HAVE BEHAVED LIKE A COWARD!

THE KING THEN SENT FOR THE CHIEF MINISTER.

GOOD JACKAL, I WAS WRONG TO MAKE SO HASTY A JUDGEMENT AGAINST YOU. PLEASE RESUME YOUR DUTIES.

O KING, FIRST YOU BESTOWED UPON ME THE HIGHEST HONOURS OF THE LAND. THEN YOU TREATED ME AS YOUR ENEMY.

I HAVE WRONGED YOU. I SHOULD HAVE JUDGED BY YOUR ACTIONS WHICH HAVE ALWAYS BEEN JUST.

TRUST ONCE LOST CANNOT BE REGAINED. SUCH A SCAR PERMANENTLY MARS RELATIONSHIPS. PLEASE GIVE ME YOUR PERMISSION TO GO AWAY.

HE THEN WENT AWAY AND SPENT THE REST OF HIS DAYS IN SOLITUDE IN THE FOREST.

18

THE SAGE AND THE DOG

IN A DENSE FOREST, INHABITED ONLY BY WILD ANIMALS, THERE ONCE LIVED A GOOD RISHI. THE WILD CREATURES LOVED HIM AND CAME TO HIM TO BE TAUGHT BY HIM.

THAT DOG IS THE MOST DEVOTED OF ALL HIS DISCIPLES!

NEVER ONCE HAS HE LEFT THE SIDE OF HIS GURU!

AND WOULD YOU BELIEVE IT? THE DOG LIVES ON NOTHING BUT FRUITS, ROOTS AND WATER!

HOW EXTRAORDINARY! ARE YOU SURE?

I AM CERTAIN! LOOK AT HIM! HE'S SO WEAK AND THIN DUE TO FASTING.

ONE DAY, IT SO HAPPENED THAT A LEOPARD STRAYED INTO THE HERMITAGE.

HUNGRY AND THIRSTY, AND HIS JAWS WIDE OPEN, THE LEOPARD LOOKED LIKE A SECOND YAMA.* AND HE WANTED TO POUNCE UPON THE DOG.

TREMBLING WITH FEAR, THE DOG TURNED TO HIS GURU.

OH HOLY ONE! THIS LEOPARD WISHES TO EAT ME! PLEASE... FIND SOME WAY OF SAVING ME!

DON'T BE AFRAID, MY SON! LET THY NATURAL FORM DISAPPEAR AND...

...BE THOU A LEOPARD!

* THE LORD OF DEATH

20

THERE WAS A BLINDING FLASH LIKE A SUN EXPLODING. THE DOG WAS TRANSFORMED INTO A LEOPARD WITH A COAT WHICH GLEAMED LIKE BURNISHED GOLD!

SEEING THIS MAGNIFICENT ANIMAL OF HIS OWN SPECIES, THE LEOPARD WHO HAD COME TO EAT HIM FLED.

SOME TIME LATER, A FIERCE TIGER CAME TO THE HERMITAGE.

GR...RR...

THE LEOPARD WHO WAS REALLY A DOG, CROUCHED IN FEAR.

WITH HIS INNER VISION, THE RISHI SENSED THE DANGER AND QUICKLY TRANSFORMED HIM INTO A POWERFUL TIGER.

SEEING THIS NEW TIGER, THE HUNGRY TIGER LEFT AT ONCE.

THE DOG, NOW TRANSFORMED INTO A REGAL TIGER, GAVE UP HIS FORMER AUSTERE DIET AND BEGAN TO SUBSIST ON OTHER ANIMALS.

ONE DAY, HAVING HAD A LARGE MEAL, HE WAS SLEEPING IN THE YARD OF THE HERMITAGE...

...WHEN A ROGUE ELEPHANT CAME THERE, LOOKING LIKE A GREY CLOUD ON A STORMY HORIZON.

AS THIS ELEPHANT OF TERRIFYING PROPORTIONS APPROACHED, THE TIGER WHO WAS FORMERLY A DOG RUSHED TO THE RISHI FOR PROTECTION.

IN AN INSTANT, THE RISHI TRANSFORMED HIM INTO A MAGNIFICENT ELEPHANT!

I MUST BE GOING MAD! I THOUGHT I WAS CHASING A TIGER BUT HE APPEARS TO BE ONE OF MY OWN SPECIES!

HA! HA! HE'S GONE!

DELIGHTED WITH HIS NEW FORM, THE RISHI'S ELEPHANT WANDERED OFF TO A NEARBY LAKE, ENJOYING THE COOL WATER.

THEN ONE DAY, A SLAYER OF ALL ANIMALS CAME TO THE SPOT. IT WAS A SHARABHA, A TERRIBLE ANIMAL WITH EIGHT LEGS AND HE MADE STRAIGHT FOR THE RISHI'S ELEPHANT!

BUT THE ELEPHANT, THROUGH THE RISHI'S GRACE, HAD BECOME A SHARABHA, TOO. ONLY HE WAS BIGGER AND MORE FIERCE THAN THE OTHER ONE!

FRIGHTENED, THE SHARABHA BEGAN TO SLINK AWAY.

NOW OUR SHARABHA POSSESSED THE FIELD. BUT, WITH THE SUCCESSIVE CHANGES, HE HAD CHANGED IN OTHER WAYS TOO. NO LONGER DID HE LIVE ON FRUITS AND ROOTS. HE WAS NOW CONFIRMED IN THE HABITS OF A CARNIVOROUS BEAST.

AND NOW, EVER THIRSTING FOR FRESH BLOOD, HE WISHED TO SLAY THE SAGE!

THE SAGE DIVINED HIS INTENTION AT ONCE.

YOU DOG! IT WAS TO ME YOU OWED YOUR TRANSFORMATIONS AS LEOPARD, TIGER, ELEPHANT! AND FINALLY, HAVING BECOME A SHARABHA, YOU WISH TO DO ME INJURY!

BE THOU A DOG AGAIN!

AS BEFORE, THE DOG RESTED AT THE FEET OF HIS GURU...

... BUT HE HAD BECOME VERY CHEERLESS. SO THE RISHI DROVE HIM AWAY.

GO AWAY, SINFUL CREATURE! NO ONE SHOULD BE PLACED IN A POSITION FOR WHICH HE IS NOT SUITED! YOU ARE CERTAINLY FIT ONLY TO BE A DOG!

THE SWAN AND THE CROW

THERE ONCE LIVED A CROW WHO WAS THE FAVOURITE OF THREE BOYS. EVERY DAY THEY FED HIM WITH THE REMNANTS OF THEIR FOOD.

COME, LOVELY CROW, WE WON'T HARM YOU!

EAT! EAT!

DOESN'T HE LOOK LOVELY?

LOOK AT HIS GLOSSY WINGS!

THE ADMIRATION OF THE CHILDREN FILLED THE CROW WITH PRIDE...

...AND HE BELIEVED HIMSELF TO BE THE HANDSOMEST, CLEVEREST BIRD IN THE LAND.

SOON HE WAS FLYING EFFORTLESSLY ACROSS THE OCEAN.

BUT THE CROW WAS SO EXHAUSTED HE COULD BARELY KEEP HIMSELF ABOVE THE WATER.

WHAT SHALL I DO? THERE IS NOT A TREE IN SIGHT! WHERE CAN I STOP TO REST?

HELP! OR I'LL DROWN!

JUST THEN THE SWAN RETURNED.

WHAT KIND OF FLYING IS THAT, FRIEND?

29

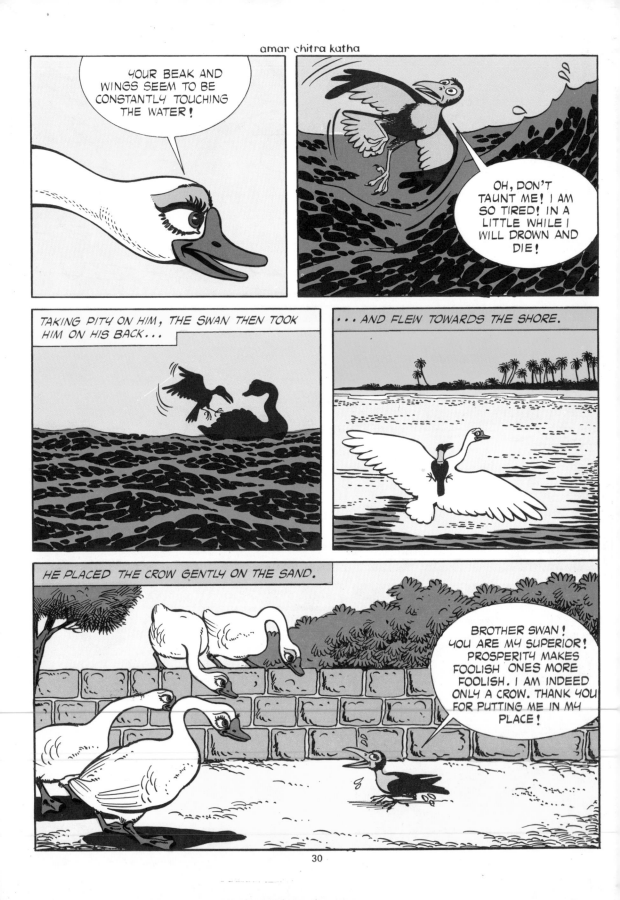

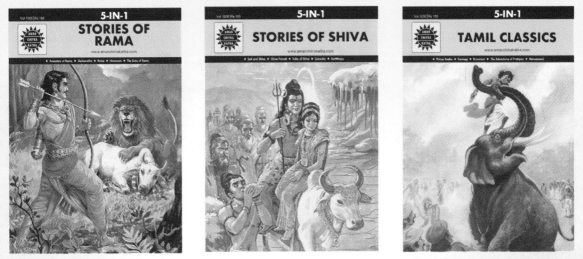

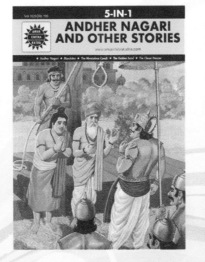